2002-03-249 Raintree

DATE DUE

Tundra Scientists

BY CHUCK MILLER

Raintree Steck-Vaughn Publishers
A Harcourt Company

Austin · New York
www.steck-vaughn.com

Published by Raintree Steck-Vaughn Publishers, an imprint of Steck-Vaughn Company.

Library of Congress Cataloging-in-Publication Data is available upon request.
ISBN: 0-7398-4752-X

Printed and bound in the United States of America
1 2 3 4 5 6 7 8 9 10 WZ 05 04 03 02 01

Produced by Compass Books

Photo Acknowledgments
Corbis, cover
Digital Stock, 14, 40 (bottom), 41 (top)
Mike Kunz, 22, 25, 26, 41 (bottom)
Photo Network/Bill Terry, title page; Mark Newman, 6; Howard Folsom, 32; Jeff Greenberg, 34
Visuals Unlimited/Steve McCutcheon, 9, 40 (top); Beth Davidson, 10; Doug Sokell, 12, 28; Will Troyer, 18; David Matherly, 30; Gerard Fueher, 39; Robert Barber, 44

Content Consultants
Maria Kent Rowell
Science Consultant, Sebastopol, California

David Larwa
National Science Education Consultant
Educational Training Services, Brighton, Michigan

This book supports the National Science Standards.

Contents

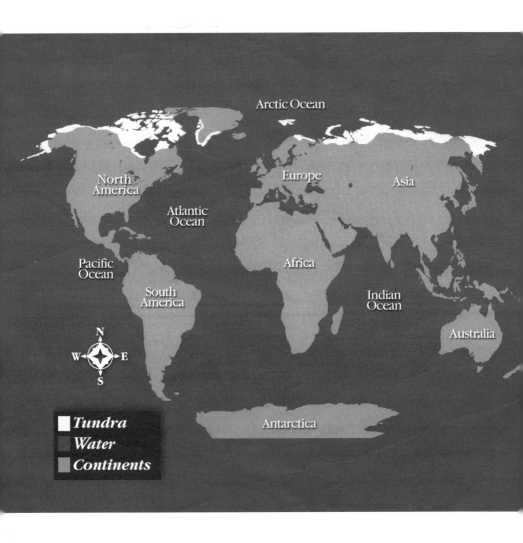

This map shows where arctic tundra is located throughout the world.

What Is a Tundra Biome?

The tundra is a **biome**. A biome is a large region, or area, made of communities. A community is a group of certain plants and animals that live in the same place.

Communities in the same biome are alike in some ways. In the tundra biome, for example, plants and animals must be able to live in a cold and dry **climate**.

The tundra is the world's coldest biome. Temperatures there can be as cold as -60° F (-50° C). There is little rainfall on the tundra. Less than 10 inches (25.4 cm) of rain falls there each year. The tundra is wet, however, because the ground is often frozen, and water cannot seep into it.

This llama is looking for food to eat on this alpine tundra in Chile.

Does snow harm plants on the tundra? No, it does not. Snow covering plants keeps them warm. Snow also keeps the wind from blowing on plants.

Kinds of Tundra

The two types of tundra biome are arctic tundra and alpine tundra. Arctic tundra is found mainly in the most northern parts of the world, in Northern Europe, Siberia, and in far northern parts of North America. It can also be found on islands in the Arctic Ocean. Alpine tundra is found at some of the world's highest places, mainly on mountains.

The word "tundra" comes from a Finnish word that means treeless plain. Many people think that all of the tundra is flat. Alpine tundra, however, is found on high mountains and is not flat at all. Arctic tundra can also have small hills on it.

What Is Tundra?

Tundra is a cold area where the ground below the surface is permanently frozen. Many people think that the tundra is always covered by snow. Tundra, though, is not always covered by snow. Many plants grow on the arctic and alpine tundra during the short warm, or growing, season.

Both kinds of tundra have a warm season and a cold season. Strong winds and heavy snows make the tundra dry during the long cold season. The warm season usually lasts only six to ten weeks. During the warm season, the ground becomes very wet in the arctic tundra. Ponds form during that time. Water sinks more easily into the soil of the alpine tundra. It is not as wet as the arctic tundra during the warm season.

Although the tundra's surface is not frozen all year round, the ground below the surface is. On the arctic tundra, the ground can freeze as far as 1,000 feet (300 m) below Earth's surface. This frozen ground is called **permafrost**. Permafrost does not allow the water to soak

▲ This photograph shows the frozen permafrost below the tundra's topsoil.

very far into it. Water evaporates slowly on the arctic tundra. **Evaporation** happens when water turns into a gas called water vapor. The slow evaporation and the permafrost are the reasons why the arctic tundra has a wet climate, even though it receives little rain.

Scientists believe glaciers, like this one, left behind rocky soil on the tundra.

FUN FACT

Do all the animals on the tundra stay there year round? No, they do not. Caribou travel long distances in search of food when the seasons change. This kind of travel is called migration.

Rocky Soil

There are many rocks in the alpine and arctic tundra's soil. Scientists think the rocks got there during an ice age. An ice age is a time in history when sheets of ice called glaciers covered a large part of Earth. The last ice age happened about 10,000 to 15,000 years ago.

Scientists believe that glaciers eroded the land as they melted. **Erosion** happens when water or wind moves over rock or soil and carries it away. Scientists believe the melting glaciers made the tundra's rocky soil this way.

This photograph shows lichen and moss, two common tundra plants.

What Plants Live on Tundra?

Tundra plants have adapted to live in the cold climate. To be adapted means that something is a good fit for where it lives. Many plants that live in tundra could not live in another biome.

The arctic tundra is home to many plants that can live in cold temperatures. They can grow in soil with few **nutrients**. Nutrients are materials that living things need to stay healthy and to grow.

Plants that live on the arctic tundra include **mosses**, grasses, sedges, **lichens**, small scrubs, and **cushion plants**. Mosses are small furry plants that do not have roots. Lichens are plants like moss that grow on rocks and also on mosses. Cushion plants grow in small clumps and look like cushions.

The alpine tundra also has plants that can live in a harsh climate. Many of the plants that live on the arctic tundra also live on the alpine tundra.

Trees cannot usually grow on the tundra because it is above the **treeline**. The treeline is the **altitude** or latitude above which no trees can grow. Much of the alpine tundra is 11,000 feet (3,350 m) above sea level. Sea level is the average level of the surface of the ocean. It is used as a starting point to measure height or depth.

Elks like this one are animals that live in the alpine tundra.

What Animals Live on Tundra?

Animals that live in the arctic tundra include arctic foxes, wolves, polar bears, and caribou. Animals that live in the alpine tundra include sheep, elk, and mountain goats. These animals all have thick fur. They have adapted to stay warm during the coldest times of the year.

Many of these animals also store extra fat in their bodies during the warm season. Their bodies turn this fat into energy to help them live during the coldest months when there is not much food.

People on the Tundra

Few people live in the tundra. Many people find the cold temperatures to be too harsh. However, some people do choose to live there. The Inuit of North America and the Laplanders of Europe and Asia live on the tundra.

Many people visit the tundra. They come to see the tundra plants and animals during the warm season. Hunters visit during the cold season. They hunt caribou and other animals.

How and why Global Warming happens

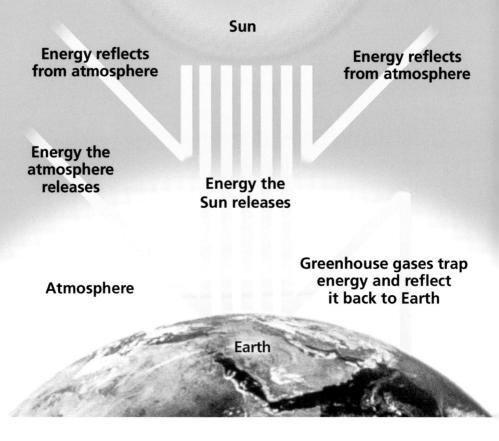

Sun

Energy reflects from atmosphere

Energy reflects from atmosphere

Energy the atmosphere releases

Energy the Sun releases

Greenhouse gases trap energy and reflect it back to Earth

Atmosphere

Earth

Why Is Tundra in Danger?

The arctic and alpine tundra are delicate places, and people can easily harm tundra habitats. A habitat is a place where an animal or plant usually lives. Permafrost on the arctic tundra can melt easily if cars or trucks are driven on it. Even just walking across tundra can hurt the soil and plants. Once they are hurt, it takes many years for soil and plants to heal.

Pollution threatens both the alpine and arctic tundra. Pollution is harmful materials that people put into the air, water, or soil. People visiting parks might throw a candy-bar wrapper on the ground. This wrapper could cover a small plant and not let it get the light it needs. The plant could die, and it might take years for a new one to grow. Pollution in the tundra soil can kill plants. Then, some caribou and elk may die because there are not enough plants to eat. Wolves and other animals that eat caribou will then not have enough to eat either.

In the past, hunters have also killed too many animals on the arctic and alpine tundra. Laws now protect endangered animals in these biomes. Endangered means in danger of becoming extinct.

Global warming can also affect tundra. Global warming is a slow but measurable rise in temperatures across all of Earth. Even small changes in temperatures can cause changes in weather patterns. These changes mean some of the tundra might receive more or less rain. This can affect the plants and animals that live there.

This picture shows what the tundra in the Arctic National Wildlife Refuge looks like from above.

Early Scientists in Alaska

O laus and Margaret "Mardy" Murie are two of the most important people to study the arctic and alpine tundra. Olaus studied plants and animals in the tundra. Mardy wrote about the tundra and told people how important it was. This husband and wife team helped start the Arctic National Wildlife Refuge in Alaska.

In college, Olaus studied zoology and wildlife biology, graduating in 1912. Zoology is the study of animals. Biology is the study of animals and plants. Between 1920 to 1926, Olaus studied caribou in Alaska. He counted caribou and watched where they traveled during different seasons. He met and married Mardy during this time and then began traveling to study and try to save different biomes.

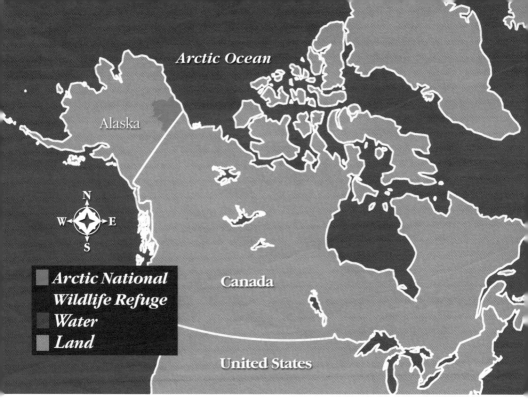

Arctic Ocean

Alaska

N
W · E
S

Arctic National
Wildlife Refuge
Water
Land

Canada

United States

 This map shows where the Arctic National
Wildlife Refuge is.

What Did the Muries Do?

In 1945, Olaus became the director of the
Wilderness Society. This group helps protect
plants and animals in different biomes all over
the world. Olaus and Mardy told people how
important the United States National Park

Service is. They told people how the service protects important biomes like the forests and tundra. People listened to Olaus and Mardy. Over time, the Muries helped the National Park Service open many new national parks.

Olaus died in 1963. Mardy, however, kept working to save the tundra. She wrote about the trips she and Olaus had taken to Alaska. She also wrote about the things Olaus had studied in Alaska.

In 1980, members of the U.S. government set aside the Arctic National Wildlife Refuge. This Alaskan refuge is made up of almost 9 million acres of arctic and alpine tundra. Many plants and animals that live there could not live anywhere else.

President Jimmy Carter thanked Mardy for the work she and Olaus have done. He said that Olaus and Mardy have helped to save the tundra in Alaska.

Kunz camps in tents far from people to study the tundra in Alaska.

A Scientist in Alaska Today

Mike Kunz works for the Alaska Bureau of Land Management. He has lived and worked in the arctic and alpine tundra of Alaska for more than 30 years. Kunz is an archaeologist and paleoecologist. Archaeology is the study of how humans lived in the past. **Paleoecology** is the study of how the climate, plants, and animals of a biome have changed over time.

Very few people live on or near the tundra in Alaska. The closest town to where Kunz lives is 200 miles (320 km) away. The closest road is 170 miles (272 km) away. Kunz says he likes working in such a harsh environment with so few people.

What Does Kunz Study?

Kunz spends much of his time studying the tundra during the summer. Where he lives, there are 24 hours of daylight during the summer. Temperatures range from 25° to 75° F (-4° to 24° C). It can snow at any time. Kunz says it often snows for a day or two at a time. He says that he must be prepared for any type of weather.

In his work, Kunz digs into the soil of the tundra to try to discover artifacts. Artifacts are things people in the past used in their daily lives. Artifacts may be tools, weapons, or things people used to eat with, such as plates and cups.

Kunz tries to understand how the people, plants, and animals that have lived on the arctic tundra have changed its climate. He also wants to know how the climate has changed the people, plants, and animals that live there. Kunz says that Earth's temperature is steadily growing warmer. "If it keeps getting warmer, the permafrost on the tundra may melt. The tundra would then start to rot and give off gases that could cause Earth to become even warmer," he says.

These scientists are working with Kunz to try to find artifacts on the tundra.

There are many animals where Kunz works.
This squirrel has entered Kunz's camp.

Dangers of Tundra Research

Kunz and the scientists he works with must
carry guns when doing research. There are
many grizzly bears where they work.

Getting food can be a problem, too. Once, a
helicopter bringing food to Kunz and the other

scientists did not show up on time. Kunz and the scientists knew that a pair of wolves raising their pups nearby had just killed a caribou. Kunz and the scientists had to cut some of the meat off the caribou after the wolves had left. They used this meat for food until the helicopter showed up a few days later.

What Is Kunz Learning?

Kunz is learning more about what the tundra was like around 12,000 years ago. He uses this information to see how the tundra has changed over time. "If we can learn how the people, plants, and animals that live on the tundra affect it," Kunz says, "we can learn how to save the tundra."

Kunz says that many people want to drill for oil in the Arctic National Wildlife Refuge in Alaska. Many plants and animals live there, though. "If people begin drilling for oil on the refuge, many of the plants and animals could be lost forever," Kunz says.

Jorgenson studies tundra plants that grow in places people do not usually look.

A Scientist in an Arctic Refuge

Janet Jorgenson is the botanist for the Arctic National Wildlife Refuge. Botany is the study of plants. Jorgenson spends many hours working in the alpine and arctic tundra, keeping track of the different plants she finds. She also looks to find new plants that no one knows about yet.

Jorgenson says studying plants makes her look at the world around her more closely. She sees tiny plants that grow on the tundra that other people might not see because they do not look closely enough.

In summary, Jorgenson studies the plants that grow during the tundra's short growing season.

Studying on Tundra

Jorgenson says computers are a useful tool for studying plants. She writes down the different plants she finds and where they grow. Then, she enters that information into a computer. She uses the computer to try to understand why some plants grow in only one area or another. She also tries to guess when and where the plants will grow.

During the summer, Jorgenson spends much of her time on the refuge at a place called the North Slope. She can see the Arctic Ocean from the mountains there. Jorgenson says the sky at the North Slope is bright blue and does not look like it ends.

Jorgenson often camps in tents when she is studying plants on the North Slope. She brings along books that help her understand the kinds of plants she finds. Jorgenson does not pick any of the plants. She knows that if she did, a new one might not grow in its place for a long time.

To keep animals, plants, and soil safe, visitors to the tundra should be careful.

What Are Other Kids Saying?

Anthony Beatty is a sixth grade student who enjoys studying the tundra. He says "science has taught me a lot about the importance of the tundra, so I think we should do all we can to save it."

Keeping Tundra Healthy

Jorgenson says that people can hurt the tundra's plants and soil very easily. In the 1980s, people drove through the land that is now the refuge to see if there might be oil there. The tire tracks are still there. "Plants cannot grow in soil where the tracks are," Jorgenson says.

Jorgenson also tells people to be careful when camping on the tundra. They might not know that their footprints or campsites might kill plants or keep them from growing.

These visitors to the tundra are keeping plants and soil safe by being careful where they walk.

What Does the Future Hold for Tundra?

The future of arctic and alpine tundra depends on people. People can help save the tundra in many ways. They can be careful when walking on the tundra when they visit it. Footsteps in soft or melting soil can damage it for a long time. Stepping on a tundra plant can kill it. It will take many years before another one can grow back.

Hunters should know the laws that protect some animals on the tundra. Many of these animals are endangered. Hunters should never kill a protected animal or more animals than the law allows.

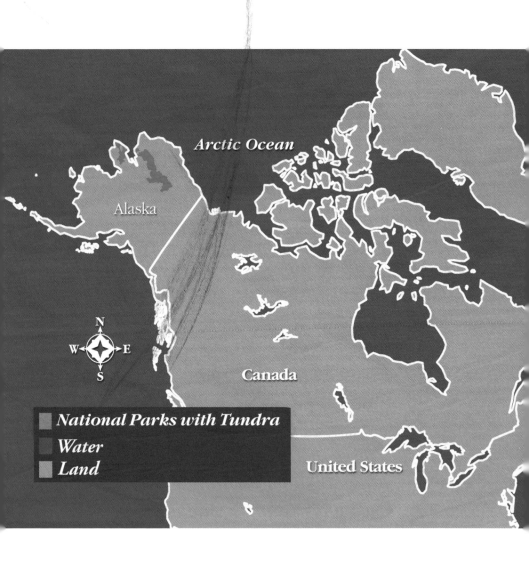

Arctic Ocean

Alaska

N
W-E
S

Canada

National Parks with Tundra
Water
Land

United States

This map shows the national parks in the United
States that contain arctic tundra.

Oil Companies and Tundra

Oil companies can also help save the tundra. These companies have to be more careful when drilling for oil in the tundra. When they build roads and camps for drilling, they kill many plants and animals.

Oil companies should look for oil in places that are not as fragile as the tundra.

Where Is Tundra Protected the Best?

Arctic and alpine tundra are protected best in national parks. A national park is land that is owned and protected by the government. At a national park, the natural habitat of the tundra is protected from damage caused by people. At many national parks, the tundra is protected from mining and drilling.

There are several national parks in the United States where people can visit tundra. One park is the Arctic National Wildlife Refuge in Alaska. People can see arctic tundra there. Another park is the Rocky Mountain National Park. People can see alpine tundra in this park.

The Endangered Polar Bear

One endangered arctic tundra animal is the polar bear. The polar bear is the world's largest land-living **carnivore**. Carnivores are animals that eat only other animals for food. The only carnivores larger than the polar bear live in the ocean. An adult male polar bear weighs from 770 to 1,430 pounds (349 to 648 kg). Standing on its hind legs, an adult male polar bear could look an elephant straight in the eyes.

Most polar bears live in Canada, Greenland, and on Russian and Norwegian islands. People drill for oil in some of these places and destroy the polar bear's habitat. Oil spills can also damage a polar bear's fur. Polar bears freeze to death if their fur is damaged by oil.

Polar bears need people's help to survive. You can help by contacting the World Wildlife Foundation. The foundation's website and address are listed in the back of this book. The foundation teaches people about saving the polar bears and other species. It also teaches people about how to save the habitat the animals live in.

Polar bears that live on the arctic tundra are an endangered species.

Quick Facts

The tundra biome is found farther north than any other biome.

The tundra biome covers 1/5 of Earth's surface.

The only trees that grow on the tundra are dwarf willow and birch trees. They usually grow to be about 4 inches (10.2 cm) tall.

 Many mosquitoes live on the tundra because it is so wet. They drink the blood of caribou and other animals.

Many animals travel in groups on the tundra. Wolves travel in groups to hunt deer and caribou.

Most young animals are born during the warm season on the tundra. They grow up quickly because the warm season is so short.

The severe weather in the tundra has helped to protect it from damage caused by people, who find it difficult to live or work there in tents.

On the following pages, you can find sources of information that tell how to help save tundra.

Glossary

altitude (AL-ti-tood)—the height of something in relation to sea level

biome (BYE-ohm)—large regions, or areas, in the world that have similar climates, soil, plants, and animals

carnivore (KAR-nuh-vor)—an animal that eats only other animals for food

climate (KLYE-mit)—the usual weather patterns in a place

cushion plants (KUSH-uhn PLANTZ)—plants that grow in small cushion-like clumps

erosion (i-ROH-zhuhn)—when water, wind, or ice pick up and carry away Earth materials

evaporation (i-VAP-uh-ray-shun)—when a liquid changes into a gas

lichen (LYE-ken)—plants like moss that grow on rocks

moss (MAWSS)—a small, furry plant that grows in damp places

nutrient (NOO-tree-uhnt)—something that is needed by living things to grow and to stay healthy

paleoecology (PALE-ee-oh-kol-uh-jee)—the study of how the climate, plants, and animals of a biome have changed over time

permafrost (PURM-uh-frawst)—permanently frozen ground

pollution (puh-LOO-shuhn)—harmful materials that damage air, water, or soil and are often made by people

treeline (TREE-line)—an imaginary line at a latitude altitude above which trees cannot grow

Internet Sites

Arctic National Wildlife Refuge
http://arctic.fws.gov/
Learn about different flowers and plants that grow on the Arctic National Wildlife Refuge.

Kids for Saving Earth
http://www.kidsforsavingearth.org
Visit this site to learn about things you can do to help improve the environment.

National Park Service
http://www.nps.gov/
Discover the special features of different national parks and where each park is located.

The World's Tundra—Biomes
http://www.ucmp.berkeley.edu/glossary/
    gloss5/biome/tundra.html
Explore the features of the tundra biome.

Useful Addresses

Arctic National Wildlife Refuge
Refuge Manager
101 12th Avenue, Room 236
Fairbanks, AK 99701

Canadian Wildlife Service
Environment Canada
Ottawa, Ontario
K1A 0H3

Institute of Arctic and Alpine Research
Campus Box 450
Boulder, CO 80309-0450

Kids for Saving Earth
P.O. Box 421118
Minneapolis, MN 55442

Books to Read

Johnson, Rebecca L. *A Walk in the Tundra.*
Minneapolis: Carolrhoda Books, 2001.
Discover the different things you would see if you took a walk around a tundra.

Mudd-Ruth, Maria. *The Tundra.* New York:
Benchmark Books, 2000.
Here you will learn about tundra features, such as the different plants and animals that live there.

Nelson, Julie. *Tundra.* Austin, TX: Steck-Vaughn, 2001.
Explore the geography, animals, and plants as well as people's affect on this biome.

Index